Tertullian

On Monogamy

Tertullian

On Monogamy

Tertullian
On Monogamy

Published by
Lighthouse Christian Publishing
SAN 257-4330
5531 Dufferin Drive
Savage, Minnesota, 55378
United States of America

www.lighthousechristianpublishing.com

Tertullian

On Monogamy.

Chapter I.—Different Views in Regard to Marriage Held by Heretics, Psychic, and Spiritualists.

Heretics do away with marriages; Psychics accumulate them. The former marry not *even* once; the latter not *only* once. What dost thou, Law of the Creator? Between alien eunuchs and thine own grooms, thou complainest as much of the over-obedience of thine own household as of the contempt of strangers. They who abuse thee, do thee equal hurt with them who use thee not. In fact, neither is such continence laudable because it is heretical, nor such license defensible because it is psychical. The former is blasphemous, the latter wanton; the former destroys the God of marriages, the latter puts Him to the blush. Among *us*, however, whom the recognition of spiritual gifts entitles to be deservedly called Spiritual, continence is as religious as license is modest; since both the one and the other are in harmony with the Creator. Continence honors the law of marriage, license tempers it; the former is not forced, the latter is regulated; the former recognizes the power of free choice, the latter recognizes a limit. We admit one marriage, just as we do one God. The law of marriage reaps an accession of honor where it is associated with shame fastness. But to the Psychics, since they receive not the Spirit, the things which are the Spirit's are not pleasing. Thus, so long as the things which are the Spirit's please them not, the things which are of the flesh will please, as being the contraries of the Spirit. "The flesh," saith (the apostle), "lusteth against the Spirit, and the Spirit against the flesh." But what will the flesh "lust" after, except what is more *of* the flesh? For which reason withal, in the beginning, it became estranged from the Spirit. "My Spirit," saith (God), "shall not permanently abide in these men eternally, for that they are flesh."

Chapter II. —The Spiritualists Vindicated from the Charge of Novelty.

And so they upbraid the discipline of monogamy with being a heresy; nor is there any other cause whence they find themselves compelled to deny the Paraclete more than the fact that they esteem Him to be the institutor of a novel discipline, and a discipline which they find most harsh: so that this is already the first ground on which we must join issue in a general handling (of the subject), whether there is room for maintaining that the Paraclete has taught any such thing as can either be charged with novelty, in opposition to catholic tradition, or with burdensomeness, in opposition to the "light burden" of the Lord.

Now concerning each point the Lord Himself has pronounced. For in saying, "I still have many things to say unto you, but ye are not yet able to bear them: when the Holy Spirit shall be come, He will lead you into all truth," He sufficiently, of course, sets before us that He will bring such (teachings) as may be esteemed alike *novel*, as having never before been published, and finally *burdensome*, as if that were the reason why they were not published. "It follows," you say, "that by this line of argument, anything you please which is novel and burdensome may be ascribed to the Paraclete, even if it has come from the adversary spirit." No, of course. For the adversary spirit would be apparent from the diversity of his preaching, beginning by adulterating the rule of faith, and so (going on to) adulterating the order of discipline; because the corruption of that which holds the first grade, (that is, of faith, which is prior to discipline,) comes first. A man must of necessity hold heretical views of God first, and then of His institution. But the Paraclete, having many things to teach fully which the Lord deferred till He came, (according to the pre-definition,) will begin by bearing emphatic witness to Christ, (as being) such as we believe (Him to be), together with the whole order of God the Creator, and will glorify Him, and will "bring to remembrance" concerning Him. And when He has thus been recognized (as the promised Comforter), on the ground of the cardinal rule, He will reveal those "many things" which appertain to disciplines; while the integrity of His preaching commands credit for these (revelations), albeit they be "novel," inasmuch as they are now in course of revelation, albeit they be "burdensome," inasmuch as not even *now* are they found bearable: (revelations), however, of none other Christ than (the One) who said that He had withal "other many things" which were to be fully taught by the Paraclete, no less burdensome to men of our own day than to them, by whom they were then "not yet able to be borne."

Chapter III. —The Question of Novelty Further Considered in Connection with the Words of the Lord and His Apostles.

But (as for the question) whether monogamy be "burdensome," let the still shameless "infirmity of the flesh" look to that: let us meantime come to an agreement as to whether it be "novel." This (even) broader assertion we make: that even if the Paraclete had in this our day definitely prescribed a virginity or continence total and absolute, so as not to permit the heat of the flesh to foam itself down even in

single marriage, even thus He would seem to be introducing nothing of "novelty;" seeing that the Lord Himself opens "the kingdoms of the heavens" to "eunuchs," as being Himself, withal, a virgin; to whom looking, the apostle also—himself too for this reason abstinent—gives the preference to continence. ("Yes"), you say, "but saving the law of marriage." Saving it, plainly, and we will see under what limitations; nevertheless already destroying it, in so far as he gives the preference to continence. "Good," he says, "(it is) for a man not to have contact with a woman." It follows that it is evil to have contact with her; for nothing is contrary to good except evil. And accordingly (he says), "It remains, that both they who have wives so be as if they have not," that it may be the more binding on them who have not to abstain from having them. He renders reasons, likewise, for so advising: that the unmarried think about God, but the married about how, in (their) marriage, each may please his (partner). And I may contend,
that what is *permitted* is not absolutely good. For what is absolutely good is not *permitted*, but needs no asking to make it lawful. Permission has its cause sometimes even in *necessity*. Finally, in this case, there is no volition on the part of him who permits marriage. For his *volition* points another way. "I *will*," he says, "that you all so be as I too (am)." And when he shows that (so to abide) is "better," what, pray, does he demonstrate himself to "will," but what he has premised is "better?" And thus, if he *permits* something other *than what* he has "willed"—permitted not voluntarily, but of necessity—he shows that what he has unwillingly granted as an indulgence is not absolutely good. Finally, when he says, "Better it is to marry than to burn," what sort of good must that be understood to be which is better than a penalty? which cannot seem "better" except when compared to a thing very bad? "Good" is that which keeps this name *per se*; without comparison—I say not with an evil, but even—with some other good: so that, even if it be compared to and overshadowed by another good, it nevertheless remains in (possession of) the name of good. If,

on the other hand, comparison with evil is the mean which obliges it to be called good; it is not so much "good" as a species of inferior evil, which, when obscured by a higher evil, is driven to the name of good. Take away, in short, the condition, so as not to say, "Better it is to marry than to burn;" and I question whether you will have the hardihood to say, "Better (it is) to marry," not adding *than what* it is better. This done, then, it becomes *not* "better;" and while not "better," not "good" either, the condition being taken away which, while making it "better" than another thing, in that sense obliges it to be considered "good." Better it is to lose one eye than two. If, however, you withdraw from the comparison of either evil, it will not be better to have one eye, because it is not even good.

What, now, if he accommodatingly grants all indulgence to marry on the ground of his own (that is, of human) sense, out of the necessity which we have mentioned, inasmuch as "better it is to marry than to burn?" In fact, when he turns to the second case, by saying, "But to the married I officially announce—not I, but the Lord"—he shows that those things which he had said above had not been (the dictates) of the Lord's authority, but of human judgment. When, however, he turns their minds back to continence, ("But I will you all so to be,") "I think, moreover," he says, "I too have the Spirit of God;" in order that, if he had granted any indulgence out of necessity, that, by the Holy Spirit's authority, he might recall. But John, too, when advising us that "we ought so to walk as the Lord withal did," of course admonished us to walk as well in accordance with sanctity of the flesh (as in accordance with His example in other respects). Accordingly, he says more manifestly: "And every (man) who hath this hope in Him makes himself chaste, just as Himself withal is chaste." For elsewhere, again, (we read): "Be ye holy, just as He withal was holy"—in the flesh, namely. For of the Spirit he would not have said (that), inasmuch as the Spirit is without any external influence recognized as "holy," nor does He wait to be admonished to sanctity, which is His proper nature. But the flesh *is taught* sanctity; and that withal, in Christ, was holy.

Therefore, if all these (considerations) obliterate the license of marrying, whether we look into the condition on which the license is granted, or the preference of continence which is imposed, why, after the apostles, could not the same Spirit, supervening for the purpose of conducting disciple hood into "all truth" through the gradations of the times (according to what the preacher says, "A time to everything"), impose by this time a final bridle upon the flesh, no longer obliquely calling us away from marriage, but openly; since now more (than ever) "the time is become wound up,"—about 160 years having elapsed since then? Would you not spontaneously ponder (thus) in your own mind: "This discipline is old, shown beforehand, even at that early date, in the Lord's flesh and will, (and) successively thereafter in both the counsels and the examples of His apostles? Of old we were destined to this sanctity. Nothing of novelty is the Paraclete introducing. What He premonished, He is (now) definitively appointing; what He deferred, He is (now) exacting." And presently, by revolving these thoughts, you will easily persuade yourself that it was much more competent to the Paraclete to preach unity of marriage, who could withal have preached its annulling; and that it is more credible that He should have tempered what it would have become Him even to have abolished, if you understand what Christ's "will" is. Herein also you ought to recognize the Paraclete in His character of Comforter, in that He excuses your infirmity from (the stringency of) an absolute continence.

Chapter IV. —Waiving Allusion to the Paraclete, Tertullian Comes to the Consideration of the Ancient Scriptures, and Their Testimony on the Subject in Hand.

Waiving, now, the mention of the Paraclete, as of some authority of our own, evolve we the common instruments of the primitive Scriptures. This very thing is demonstrable by us: that the rule of monogamy is neither novel nor strange, nay rather, is both ancient, and proper to Christians; so that you may be sensible that the Paraclete is rather its *re*stitutor than *in*stitutor. As for what pertains to antiquity, what more ancient formal type can be brought forward, than the very original fount of the human race? One female did God fashion for the male, culling one rib of his, and (of course) (one) out of a plurality. But, moreover, in the introductory speech which preceded the work itself, He said, "It is not good for the man that he be alone; let us make a help-meet for him." For He would have said "helpers" if He had destined him to have more wives (than one). He added, too, a law concerning the future; if, that is, (the words) "And two shall be (made) into one flesh"—not three, nor more; else they would be no more "two" if (there were) more—were prophetically uttered. The law stood (firm). In short, the unity of marriage lasted to the very end in the case of the authors of our race; not because there were no other women, but because the reason *why* there were none was that the first-fruits of the race might not be contaminated by a double marriage. Otherwise, had God (so) willed, there *could* withal have been (others); at all events, he might have taken from the abundance of his own daughters—having no less an Eve (taken) out of his own bones and flesh—if piety had allowed it to be done. But where the first crime (is found) homicide, inaugurated in fratricide—no crime was so worthy of the second place as a double marriage. For it makes no difference whether a man have had two wives singly, or whether individuals (taken) at the same time have made two. The number of (the individuals) conjoined and separate is the same. Still, God's institution, after once for all suffering violence through Lamech, remained firm to the very end of that race. Second Lamech there arose none, in the way of being husband to two wives. What Scripture does not note, it denies. Other iniquities provoke the deluge: (iniquities) once for all avenged, whatever was their nature; not, however, "seventy-seven times," which (is the vengeance which) double marriages have deserved.

But again: the reformation of the second human race is traced from monogamy as its mother. Once more, "two (joined) into one flesh" undertake (the duty of) "growing and multiplying,"—Noah, (namely), and his wife, and their sons, in single marriage. Even in the very animals monogamy is recognized, for fear that even beasts should be born of adultery. "Out of all beasts," said (God), "out of all flesh, two shalt thou lead into the ark, that they may live with thee, male and female: they shall be (taken) from all flying animals according to (their) kind, and from all creepers of the earth according to their kind; two out of all shall enter unto thee, male and female." In the same formula, too, He orders sets of sevens, made up of pairs, to be gathered to him, consisting of male and female—one male and one female. What more shall I say? Even unclean birds were not allowed to enter with two females each.

Chapter V.—Connection of These Primeval Testimonies with Christ.

Thus far for the testimony of things primordial, and the sanction of our origin, and the prejudgment of the divine institution, which of course is a law, not (merely) a memorial inasmuch as, if it was "so done from the beginning," we find ourselves directed to the beginning by Christ: just as, in the question of divorce, by saying that that had been permitted by Moses on account of their hard-heartedness but from the beginning it had not been so, He doubtless recalls to "the beginning" the (law of) the individuity of marriage. And accordingly, those whom God "from the beginning" conjoined, "two into one flesh," man shall not at the present day separate. The apostle, too, writing to the Ephesians, says that God "had proposed in Himself, at the dispensation of the fulfilment of the times, to recall to the head" (that is, to the beginning) "things universal in Christ, which are above the heavens and above the earth in Him." So, too, the two letters of Greece, the first and the last, the Lord assumes to Himself, as figures of the beginning and end! which concur in Himself: so that, just as Alpha rolls on till it reaches Omega, and again Omega rolls back till it reaches Alpha, in the same way He might show that in Himself is both the downward course of the beginning on to the end, and the backward course of the end up to the beginning; so that every economy, ending in Him through whom it began,—through the Word of God, that is, who was made flesh,—may have an end correspondent to its beginning. And so truly in Christ are all things recalled to "the beginning," that even faith returns from circumcision to the integrity of that (original) flesh, as "it was from the beginning;" and freedom of meats and abstinence from blood alone, as "it was from the beginning;" and the individuality of marriage, as "it was from the beginning;" and the restriction of divorce, which *was not* "from the beginning;" and lastly, the whole man into Paradise, where he was "from the beginning." Why, then, ought He not to restore Adam thither at least as a monogamist, who cannot present him in so entire perfection as he was when dismissed thence? Accordingly, so far as pertains to the restitution of the beginning, the logic both of the dispensation you live under, and of your hope, exact this from you, that what was "from the beginning" (should be) in accordance with "the beginning;" which (beginning) you find counted in Adam, and recounted in Noah. Make your election, in which of the twain you account your "beginning." In both, the censorial power of monogamy claims you for itself. But again: if the beginning passes on to the end (as Alpha to Omega), as the end passes back to the beginning (as Omega to Alpha), and thus our origin is transferred to Christ, the animal to the spiritual—inasmuch as "(that was) not first which is spiritual, but (that) which (is) animal; then what (is) spiritual,"—let us, in like manner (as before), see whether you owe this very (same) thing to this second origin also: whether the last Adam also meet you in the selfsame form as the first; since the last Adam (that is, Christ) was entirely unwedded, as was even the first Adam before his exile. But, presenting to your weakness the gift of the example of His own flesh, the more perfect Adam—that is, Christ, more perfect on this account as well (as on others), that He was more entirely pure—stands before you, if you are willing (to copy Him), as a voluntary celibate in the flesh. If, however, you are unequal (to that perfection), He stands before you a monogamist in spirit, having one Church as His spouse, according to the figure of Adam and of Eve, which (figure) the apostle interprets of that great sacrament of Christ and the Church, (teaching that), through the spiritual, it was analogous to the carnal monogamy. You see, therefore, after what manner, renewing your origin even in Christ, you cannot trace down that (origin) without the profession of monogamy; unless, (that is), you be in flesh what He is in spirit; albeit withal, what He was in flesh, you equally ought to have been.

Chapter VI. —The Case of Abraham, and Its Bearing on the Present Question.

But let us proceed with our inquiry into some eminent chief fathers of our origin: for there are some to whom our monogamist parents Adam and Noah are not pleasing, nor perhaps Christ either. To Abraham, in fine, they appeal; prohibited though they are to acknowledge any other father than God. Grant, now, that Abraham is our father; grant, too, that Paul is. "In the Gospel," says he, "I have begotten you." Show yourself a son even of Abraham. For your origin in him, you must know, is not referable to every period of his life: there is a definite time at which he is your father. For if "faith" is the source whence we are reckoned to Abraham as his "sons" (as the apostle teaches, saying to the Galatians, "You know, consequently, that (they) who are of faith, these are sons of Abraham"), *when* did Abraham "believe God and it was accounted to him for righteousness?" I suppose when still in monogamy, since (he was) not yet in circumcision. But if afterwards he changed to either (opposite)—to digamy through cohabitation with his handmaid, and to circumcision through the seal of the testament—you cannot acknowledge him as your father except at that time when he "believed God," if it is true that it is according to *faith* that you are his son, not according to *flesh*. Else, if it be the later Abraham whom you follow as your father—that is, the digamist (Abraham)—receive him withal in his circumcision. If you reject his circumcision, it follows that you will refuse his digamy too. Two characters of his mutually diverse in two several ways, you will not be able to blend. His digamy began with circumcision, his monogamy with uncircumcision. You receive digamy; admit circumcision too. You retain uncircumcision; you are bound to monogamy too. Moreover, so true is it that it is of the monogamist Abraham that you are the son, just as of the uncircumcised, that if you be circumcised you immediately cease to be his son, inasmuch as you will not be "of faith," but of the *seal* of a faith which had been justified in uncircumcision. You have the apostle: learn (of him), together with the Galatians. In like manner, too, if you have involved yourself in digamy, you are not the son of that Abraham whose "faith" preceded in monogamy. For albeit it is subsequently that he is called "a father of many nations," still it is of *those* (nations) who, as the fruit of the "faith" which precedes digamy, had to be accounted "sons of Abraham."

Thenceforward let matters see to themselves. Figures are one thing; laws another. Images are one thing; statutes another. Images pass away when fulfilled: statutes remain permanently to be fulfilled. Images prophesy: statutes govern. What that digamy of Abraham portends, the same apostle fully teaches, the interpreter of each testament, just as he likewise lays it down that our "seed" is called in Isaac. If you are "of the free woman," and belong to Isaac, he, at all events, maintained unity of marriage to the last.

These accordingly, I suppose, are they in whom my origin is counted. All others I ignore. And if I glance around at their examples—(examples) of some David heaping up marriages for himself even through sanguinary means, of some Solomon rich in wives as well as in other riches—you are bidden to "follow the better things;" and you have withal Joseph but once wedded, and on this score I venture to say better than his father; you have Moses, the intimate eye-witness of God; you have Aaron the chief priest. The second Moses, also, of the second People, who led our representatives into the (possession of) the promise of God, in whom the Name (of Jesus) was first inaugurated, was no digamist.

Chapter VII. —From Patriarchal, Tertullian Comes to Legal, Precedents.

After the ancient examples of the patriarchs, let us equally pass on to the ancient documents of the legal Scriptures, that we may treat in order of all our canon. And since there are some who sometimes assert that they have nothing to do with the law (which Christ has not dissolved, but fulfilled), sometimes catch at such parts of the law as they choose; plainly do we too assert that the law has deceased in this sense, that its burdens—according to the sentence of the apostles—which not even the fathers were able to sustain, have wholly ceased: such (parts), however, as relate to righteousness not only permanently remain reserved, but even amplified; in order, to be sure, that our righteousness may be able to redound above the righteousness of the scribes and of the Pharisees. If "righteousness" must, of course chastity must too. If, then, forasmuch as there is in the law a precept that a man is to take in marriage the wife of his brother if he has died without children, for the purpose of raising up seed to his brother; and this may happen repeatedly to the same person, according to that crafty question of the Sadducees; men for that reason think that frequency of marriage is permitted in other cases as well: it will be their duty to understand first the reason of the precept itself; and thus they will come to know that that reason, now ceasing, is among those parts of the law which have been cancelled. Necessary it was that there should be a succession to the marriage of a brother if he died childless: first, because that ancient benediction, "Grow and multiply," had still to run its course; secondly, because the sins of the fathers used to be exacted even from the sons; thirdly, because eunuchs and barren persons used to be regarded as ignominious. And thus, for fear that such as had died childless, not from natural inability, but from being prematurely overtaken by death, should be judged equally accursed (with the other class); for this reason, a vicarious and (so to say) posthumous offspring used to be supplied them. But (now), when the "extremity of the times" has cancelled (the command) "Grow and multiply," since the apostles (another command), "It remained, that both they who have wives so be as if they have not," because "the time is compressed;" and "the sour grape" chewed by "the fathers" has ceased "to set the sons' teeth on edge," for, "each one shall die in his own sin;" and "eunuchs" not only have lost ignominy, but have even deserved grace, being invited into "the kingdoms of the heavens:" the law of succeeding to the wife of a brother being buried, its contrary has obtained—that of *not* succeeding to the wife of a brother. And thus, as we have said before, what has ceased to be valid, on the cessation of its reason, cannot furnish a ground of argument to another. Therefore, a wife, when her husband is dead, will not marry; for if she marries, she will of course be marrying (his) brother: for "all we are brethren." Again, the woman, if intending to marry, has to marry "in the Lord;" that is, not to a heathen, but to a brother, inasmuch as even the ancient law forbids marriage with members of another tribe. Since, moreover, even in Leviticus there is a caution, "Whoever shall have taken (his) brother's wife, (it) is uncleanness—turpitude; without children shall (he) die;" beyond doubt, while the man is prohibited from marrying a second time, the woman is prohibited too, having no one to marry except a brother. In what way, then, an agreement shall be established between the apostle and the Law (which he is not impugning in its entirety), shall be shown when we shall have come to his own epistle. Meantime, so far as pertains to the law, the lines of argument drawn from it are more suitable for us (than for our opponents). In short, the same (law) prohibits priests from marrying a second time. The daughter also of a priest it bids, if widowed or repudiated, if she has had no seed, to return into her father's home and be nourished from his bread. The reason why (it is said), "If she has had no seed," is not that if she has she may marry again—for how much more will she abstain from marrying if she has sons? —but that, if she has, she may be "nourished" by her son rather than by her father; in order that the son, too, may carry out the precept of God, "Honor father and mother." Us, moreover, Jesus, the Father's Highest and Great Priest, clothing us from His own store—inasmuch as they "who are baptized in Christ have put on Christ"—has made "priests to God His Father," according to John. For the reason why He recalls that young man who was hastening to his father's obsequies, is that He may show that we are called priests by Him; (priests) whom the Law used to forbid to be present at the sepulture of parents: "Over every dead soul," it says, "the priest shall not enter, and over his own father and over his own mother he shall not be contaminated."

"Does it follow that we too are bound to observe *this* prohibition?" No, of course. For our one Father, God, *lives*, and our mother, the Church; and neither are we dead who live to God, nor do we bury our dead, inasmuch as they too are living in Christ. At all events, priests we are called by Christ; debtors to monogamy, in accordance with the pristine Law of God, which prophesied at that time of us in its own priests.

Chapter VIII. —From the Law Tertullian Comes to the Gospel. He Begins with Examples Before Proceeding to Dogmas.

Turning now to the law, which is properly ours—that is, to the Gospel—by what kind of examples are we met, until we come to definite dogmas? Behold, there immediately present themselves to us, on the threshold as it were, the two priestesses of Christian sanctity, Monogamy and Continence: one modest, in Zechariah the priest; one absolute, in John the forerunner: one appeasing God; one preaching Christ: one proclaiming a perfect priest; one exhibiting "more than a prophet,"—him, namely, who has not only preached or personally pointed out, but even baptized Christ. For who was more worthily to perform the initiatory rite on the body of the Lord, than flesh similar in kind to that which conceived and gave birth to that (body)? And indeed it was a virgin, about to marry once for all after her delivery, who gave birth to Christ, in order that each title of sanctity might be fulfilled in Christ's parentage, by means of a mother who was both virgin, and wife of one husband. Again, when He is presented as an infant in the temple, who is it who receives Him into his hands? who is the first to recognize Him in spirit? A man "just and circumspect," and of course no digamist, (which is plain) even (from this consideration), lest (otherwise) Christ should presently be more worthily preached by a woman, an aged widow, and "the wife of one man;" who, living devoted to the temple, was (already) giving in her own person a sufficient token what sort of persons ought to be the adherents to the spiritual temple, —that is, the Church. Such eye-witnesses the Lord in infancy found; no different ones had He in adult age. Peter alone do I find—through (the mention of) his "mother-in-law", —to have been married. Monogamist I am led to presume him by consideration of the Church, which, built upon him, was destined to appoint every grade of her Order from monogamists. The rest, while I do not find them married, I must of necessity understand to have been either eunuchs or continent. Nor indeed, if, among the Greeks, in accordance with the carelessness of custom, women and wives are classed under a common name—however, there is a name proper to *wives*—shall we therefore so interpret Paul as if he demonstrates the apostles to have had wives? For if he were disputing about marriages, as he does in the sequel, where the apostle could better have named some particular example, it would appear right for him to say, "For have we not the power of leading about *wives*, like the other apostles and Cephas?" But when he subjoins those (expressions) which show his abstinence from (insisting on) the supply of maintenance, saying, "For have we not the power of eating and drinking?" he does not demonstrate that "wives" were led about by the apostles, whom even such as have not still have the power of eating and drinking; but simply "women," who used to minister to them in the same way (as they did) when accompanying the Lord. But further, if Christ reproves the scribes and Pharisees, sitting in the official chair of Moses, but not doing what they taught, what kind of (supposition) is it that He Himself withal should set upon His own official chair men who were mindful rather to enjoin—(but) not likewise to practice—sanctity of the flesh, which (sanctity) He had in all ways recommended to their teaching and practicing? —first by His own example, then by all other arguments; while He tells (them) that "the kingdom of heavens" is "children's;" while He associates with these (children) others who, after marriage, remained (or became) virgins;" while He calls (them) to (copy) the simplicity of the dove, a bird not merely innocuous, but modest too, and whereof one male knows one female; while He denies the Samaritan woman's (partner to be) a husband, that He may show that manifold husbandry is adultery; while, in the revelation of His own glory, He prefers, from among so many saints and prophets, to have with him Moses and Elias—the one a monogamist, the other a voluntary celibate (for Elias was nothing else than John, who came "in the power and spirit of Elias"); while that "man gluttonous and toping," the "frequenter of luncheons and suppers, in the company of publicans and sinners," sups once for all at a single marriage, though, of course, many were marrying (around Him); for He willed to *attend* (marriages) only so often as (He willed) them to *be*.

Chapter IX. —From Examples Tertullian Passes to Direct Dogmatic Teachings. He Begins with the Lord's Teaching.

But grant that these argumentations may be thought to be forced and founded on conjectures, if no dogmatic teachings have stood parallel with them which the Lord uttered in treating of divorce, which, permitted formerly, He now prohibits, first because "from the beginning it was not so," like plurality of marriage; secondly, because "What God hath conjoined, man shall not separate,"—for fear, namely, that he contravene the Lord: for He alone shall "separate" who has "conjoined" (separate, moreover, not through the harshness of divorce, which (harshness) He censures and restrains, but through the debt of death) if, indeed, "one of two sparrows falleth not on the ground without the Father's will." Therefore, if those whom God has conjoined man shall not separate by divorce, it is equally congruous that those whom God has separated by death man is not to conjoin by marriage; the joining of the separation will be just as contrary to God's will as would have been the separation of the conjunction.

So far as regards the non-*de*struction of the will of God, and the *re*struction of the law of "the beginning." But another reason, too, conspires; nay, not another, but (one) which imposed the law of "the beginning," and moved the will of God to prohibit divorce: the fact that (he) who shall have dismissed his wife, except on the ground of adultery, makes her commit adultery; and (he) who shall have married a (woman) dismissed by her husband, of course commits adultery. A divorced woman cannot even marry legitimately; and if she commits any such act without the name of marriage, does it not fall under the category of adultery, in that adultery is crime in the way of marriage? Such is God's verdict, within straiter limits than men's, that universally, whether through marriage or promiscuously, the admission of a second man (to intercourse) is pronounced adultery by Him. For let us see what marriage is in the eye of God; and thus we shall learn what adultery equally is. Marriage is (this): when God joins "two into one flesh;" or else, finding (them already) joined in the same flesh, has given His seal to the conjunction. Adultery is (this): when, the two having been—in whatsoever way—*dis*joined, other—nay, rather alien—flesh is mingled (with either): flesh concerning which it cannot be affirmed, "This is flesh out of my flesh, and this bone out of my bones." For this, once for all done and pronounced, as from the beginning, so now too, cannot apply to "other" flesh. Accordingly, it will be without cause that you will say that God wills not a divorced woman to be joined to another man "while her husband liveth," as if He do will it "when he is dead;" whereas if she is not bound to him when dead, no more is she when living. "Alike when divorce dissevers marriage as when death does, she will not be bound to him by whom the binding medium has been broken off." To whom, then, will she be bound? In the eye of God, it matters naught whether she marry during her life or after his death. For it is not against him that she sins, but against herself. "Any sin which a man may have committed is external to the body; but (he) who commits adultery sins against his own body." But—as we have previously laid down above—whoever shall intermingle with himself "other" flesh, over and above that pristine flesh which God either conjoined into two or else found (already) conjoined, commits adultery. And the reason why He has abolished divorce, which "was not from the beginning," is, that He may strengthen that which "was from the beginning"—the permanent conjunction, (namely), of "two into one flesh:" for fear that necessity or opportunity for a *third* union of flesh may make an irruption (into His dominion); permitting divorce to no cause but one—if, (that is), the (evil) against which precaution is taken chance to have occurred beforehand. So true, moreover, is it that divorce "was not from the beginning," that among the Romans it is not till after the six hundredth year from the building of the city that this kind of "hard-heartedness" is set down as having been committed. But *they* indulge in promiscuous adulteries, even without divorcing (their partners): to *us*, even if we do divorce them, even marriage will not be lawful.

Chapter X.—St. Paul's Teaching on the Subject.

From this point I see that we are challenged by an appeal to the apostle; for the easier apprehension of whose meaning we must all the more earnestly inculcate (the assertion), that a woman is more bound when her husband is dead not to admit (to marriage) another husband. For let us reflect that divorce either is caused by discord, or else causes discord; whereas death is an event resulting from the law of God, not from an offence of man; and that it is a debt which all owe, even the unmarried. Therefore, if a divorced woman, who has been separated (from her husband) in soul as well as body, through discord, anger, hatred, and the causes of these—injury, or contumely, or whatsoever cause of complaint—is bound to a personal enemy, not to say a husband, how much more will one who, neither by her own nor her husband's fault, but by an event resulting from the Lord's law, has been—not separated from, but left behind by—her consort, be his, even when dead, to whom, even when dead, she owes (the debt of) concord? From him from whom she has heard no (word of) divorce she does not turn away; with him she is, to whom she has written no (document of) divorce; him whom she was unwilling to have lost, she retains. She has within her the license of the mind, which represents to a man, in imaginary enjoyment, all things which he has not. In short, I ask the woman herself, "Tell me, sister, have you sent your husband before you (to his rest) in peace?" What will she answer? (Will she say), "In discord?" In that case she is the more bound to him with whom she has a cause (to plead) at the bar of God. She who is bound (to another) has not departed (from him). But (will she say), "In peace?" In that case, she must necessarily persevere in that (peace) with him whom she will no longer have the power to divorce; not that she would, even if she had been able to divorce him, have been marriageable. Indeed, she prays for his soul, and requests refreshment for him meanwhile, and fellowship (with him) in the first resurrection; and she offers (her sacrifice) on the anniversaries of his falling asleep. For, unless she does these deeds, she has in the true sense divorced him, so far as in her lies; and indeed the more iniquitously—inasmuch as (she did it) as far as *was* in her power—because she had *no* power (to do it); and with the more indignity, inasmuch as it is with more indignity if (her reason for doing it is) because he did *not* deserve it. Or else shall we, pray, cease to be after death, according to (the teaching of) some Epicurus, and not according to (that of) Christ? But if we believe the resurrection of the dead, of course we shall be bound to them with whom we are destined to rise, to render an account the one of the other. "But if 'in that age they will neither marry nor be given in marriage, but will be equal to angels,' is not the fact that there will be no restitution of the conjugal relation a reason why we shall *not* be bound to our departed consorts?" Nay, but the more shall we *be* bound (to them), because we are destined to a better estate—destined (as we are) to rise to a spiritual consort ship, to recognize as well our own selves as them who are ours. Else how shall we sing thanks to God to eternity, if there shall remain in us no sense and memory of this debt; if we shall be *re*-formed in substance, not in consciousness? Consequently, we who shall be with God shall be together; since we shall all be with the one God—albeit the wages be various, albeit there be "many mansions", in the house of the same Father having labored for the "one penny" of the self-same hire, that is, of eternal life; in which (eternal life) God will still less separate them whom He has conjoined, than in this lesser life He forbids them to be separated.

Since this is so, how will a woman have room for another husband, who is, even to futurity, in the possession of her own? (Moreover, we speak to each sex, even if our discourse address itself but to the one; inasmuch as one discipline is incumbent [on both].) She will have one in spirit, one in flesh. This will be adultery, the conscious affection of one woman for two men. If the one has been disjoined from her flesh, but remains in her heart—in that place where even cogitation without carnal contact achieves beforehand both adultery by concupiscence, and matrimony by volition—he is to this hour her husband, possessing the very thing which is the mean whereby he became so—her mind, namely, in which withal, if another shall find a habitation, this will be a crime. Besides, excluded he is not, if he *has* withdrawn from viler carnal commerce. A more honorable husband is he, in proportion as he is become purer.

Chapter XI. —Further Remarks Upon St. Paul's Teaching.

Grant, now, that you marry "in the Lord," in accordance with the law and the apostle—if, notwithstanding, you care even about this—with what face do you request (the solemnizing of) a matrimony which is unlawful to those of whom you request it; of a monogamist bishop, of presbyters and deacons bound by the same solemn engagement, of widows whose Order you have in your own person refused? And they, plainly, will give husbands and wives as they would morsels of bread; for this is their rendering of "To everyone who asketh thee thou shalt give!" And they will join you together in a virgin church, the one betrothed of the one Christ! And you will pray for your *husbands*, the new and the old. Make your election, to which of the twain you will play the adulteress. I think, to both. But if you have any wisdom, be silent on behalf of the dead one. Let your silence be to him a divorce, already endorsed in the dotal gifts of another. In this way you will earn the new husband's favor, if you forget the old. You ought to take more pains to please him for whose sake you have not preferred to please God! Such (conduct) the Psychics will have it the apostle approved, or else totally failed to think about, when he wrote: "The woman is bound for such length of time as her husband lives; but if he shall have died, she is free; whom she will let her marry, only in the Lord." For it is out of this passage that they draw their defense of the license of second marriage; nay, even of (marriages) to any amount, if of second (marriage): for that which has ceased to *be once for all*, is open to *any and every number*. But the sense in which the apostle did write will be apparent, if first an agreement be come to that he did *not* write it in the sense of which the Psychics avail themselves. Such an agreement, moreover, will be come to if one first recall to mind those (passages) which are diverse from the passage in question, when tried by the standard of doctrine, of volition, and of Paul's own discipline. For, if he permits second nuptials, which were *not* "from the beginning," how does he affirm that all things are being recollected *to* the beginning in Christ? If he wills us to iterate conjugal connections, how does he maintain that "our seed is called" in the but once married

Isaac as its author? How does he make monogamy the base of his disposition of the whole Ecclesiastical Order, if this rule does not antecedently hold good in the case of laics, from whose ranks the Ecclesiastical Order proceeds? How does he call away from the enjoyment of marriage such as are still in the married position, saying that "the time is wound up," if he calls back again into marriage such as through death had escaped from marriage? If these (passages) are diverse from that one about which the present question is, it will be agreed (as we have said) that he did not write in that sense of which the Psychics avail themselves; inasmuch as it is easier (of belief) that that one passage should have some explanation agreeable with the others, than that an apostle should seem to have taught (principles)mutually diverse. That explanation we shall be able to discover in the subject-matter itself. What was the subject-matter which led the apostle to write such (words)? The inexperience of a new and just rising Church, which he was rearing, to wit, "with milk," not yet with the "solid food" of stronger doctrine; inexperience so great, that that infancy of faith prevented them from yet knowing what they were to do in regard of carnal and sexual necessity. The very phases themselves of this (inexperience) are intelligible from (the apostle's) rescripts, when he says: "But concerning these (things) which ye write; good it is for a man not to touch a woman; but, on account of fornications, let each one have his own wife." He shows that there were who, having been "apprehended by the faith" in (the state of) marriage, were apprehensive that it might not be lawful for them thenceforward to enjoy their marriage, because they had believed on the holy flesh of Christ. And yet it is "by way of allowance" that he makes the concession, "not by way of command;" that is, indulging, not enjoining, the practice. On the other hand, he "willed rather" that all should be what he himself was. Similarly, too, in sending a rescript on (the subject of) divorce, he demonstrates that some had been thinking over that also, chiefly because withal they did not

suppose that they were to persevere, after faith, in heathen marriages. They sought counsel, further, "concerning virgins"—for "precept of the Lord" there was none— (and were told) that "it is good for a man if he so remains permanently;" ("so"), of course, as he may have been found by the faith. "Thou hast been bound to a wife, seek not loosing; thou hast been loosed from a wife, seek not a wife." "But if thou shalt have taken to (thyself) a wife, thou hast not sinned;" because to one who, before believing, had been "loosed from a wife," she will not be counted a *second* wife who, subsequently to believing, is the *first*: for it is from (the time of our) believing
that our life itself dates its origin. But here he says that he "is sparing them;" else "pressure of the flesh" would shortly follow, in consequence of the straits of the times, which
shunned the encumbrances of marriage: yea, rather solicitude must be felt about earning the Lord's favor than a husband's. And thus he recalls his permission. So, then, in the very same passage in which he definitely rules that "each one ought permanently to remain in that calling in which he shall be called;" adding, "A woman is bound so long as her husband
lives; but if he shall have fallen asleep, she is free: whom she shall wish let her marry, only in the Lord," he hence also demonstrates that such a woman is to be understood as has
withal herself been "found" (by the faith) "loosed from a husband," similarly as the husband "loosed from a wife"—the "loosing" having taken place through death, of course, not through divorce; inasmuch as to the *divorced* he would grant no permission to marry, in the teeth of the primary precept. And so "a woman, if she shall have married, will not sin;" because he will not be reckoned a second husband who is, subsequently to her believing, the first, any more (than a wife thus taken will be counted a second wife). And so truly is this the case, that he *therefore* adds, "only in the Lord;" because the question in agitation was about her who had had a *heathen* (husband), and had believed *subsequently to losing him*: for

fear, to wit, that she might presume herself able to marry a heathen even *after* believing; albeit not even *this* is an object of care to the Psychics. Let us plainly know that, in the Greek original, it does not stand in the form which (through the either crafty or simple alteration of two syllables) has gone out into common use, "But if her husband *shall have* fallen asleep," as if it were speaking of the future, and thereby seemed to pertain to her who has lost her husband when already in a believing state. If this indeed had been so, license let loose without limit would have granted a (fresh) husband as often as one had been lost, without any such modesty in marrying as is congruous even to heathens. But even if it had been so, as if referring to future time, "If any (woman's) husband *shall have* died, even the future would just as much pertain to her whose husband shall die before she believed. Take it which way you will, provided you do not overturn the rest. For since these (other passages) agree to the sense (given above): "Thou hast been called (as) a slave; care not:" "Thou hast been called in uncircumcision; be not circumcised:" "Thou hast been called in circumcision; become not uncircumcised:" with which concurs, "Thou hast been bound to a wife; seek not loosing: thou hast been loosed from a wife; seek not a wife,"—manifest enough it is that these passages pertain to such as, finding themselves in a new and recent "calling," were consulting (the apostle) on the subject of those (circumstantial conditions) in which they had been "apprehended" by the faith.

This will be the interpretation of that passage, to be examined as to whether it be congruous with the time and the occasion, and with the examples and arguments preceding as well as with the sentences and senses succeeding, and primarily with the individual advice and practice of the apostle himself: for nothing is so much to be guarded as (the care) that no one be found self-contradictory.

Chapter XII. —The Explanation of the Passage Offered by the Psychics Considered.

Listen, withal, to the very subtle argumentation on the contrary side. "So true is it," say (our opponents), "that the apostle has permitted the iteration of marriage, that it is only such as are in the Clerical Order that he has stringently bound to the yoke of monogamy. For that which he prescribes to certain (individuals) he does not prescribe to all." Does it then follow, too, that to bishops alone he does *not* prescribe what he does enjoin upon all; if what he does prescribe to bishops he does *not* enjoin upon all? or is it *therefore* to all *because* to bishops? and *therefore* to bishops *because* to all? For whence is it that the bishops and clergy come? Is it not from *all*? If *all* are not bound to monogamy, whence are monogamists (to be taken) into the clerical rank? Will some separate order of monogamists have to be instituted, from which to make selection for the clerical body? (No); but when we are extolling and inflating ourselves in opposition to the clergy, then "we are all one:" then "we are all priests, because He hath made us priests to (His) God and Father." When we are challenged to a thorough equalization with the sacerdotal discipline, we lay down the (priestly) fillets, and (still) are on a par! The question in hand (when the apostle was writing), was with reference to Ecclesiastical Orders—what son of men ought to be ordained. It was therefore fitting that all the form of the common discipline should be set forth on its forefront, as an edict to be in a certain sense universally and carefully attended to, that the laity might the better know that they must themselves observe that order which was indispensable to their overseers; and that even the office of honor itself might not flatter itself in anything tending to license, as if on the ground of privilege of position. The Holy Spirit foresaw that some would say, "All things are lawful to bishops;" just as that bishop of Utina of yours feared not even the Scantinian law. Why, how many digamists, too, preside in your churches;

insulting the apostle, of course: at all events, not blushing when these passages are read under their presidency!

Come, now, you who think that an exceptional law of monogamy is made with reference to bishops, abandon withal your remaining disciplinary titles, which, together with monogamy, are ascribed to bishops. Refuse to be "irreprehensible, sober, of good morals, orderly, hospitable, easy to be taught;" nay, indeed, (be) "given to wine, prompt with the hand to strike, combative, money-loving, not ruling your house, nor caring for your children's discipline,"—no, nor "courting good renown even from strangers." For if bishops have a law of their own teaching monogamy, the other (characteristics) likewise, which will be the fitting concomitants of monogamy, will have been written (exclusively) for bishops. With laics, however, to whom monogamy is not suitable, the other (characteristics) also have nothing to do. (Thus), Psychic, you have (if you please) evaded the bonds of discipline in its entirety! Be consistent in prescribing, that "what is enjoined upon certain (individuals) is not enjoined upon all;" or else, if the other (characteristics) indeed are common, but monogamy is imposed upon bishops alone, (tell me), pray, whether *they* alone are to be pronounced *Christians* upon whom is conferred the entirety of discipline?

Chapter XIII. —Further Objections from St. Paul Answered.

"But again, writing to Timotheus, he 'wills the very young (women) to marry, bear children, act the housewife.'" He is (here) directing (his speech) to such as he denotes above— "very young widows," who, after being, "apprehended" in widowhood, and (subsequently) wooed for some length of time, after they have had Christ in their affections, "wish to marry, having judgment, because they have rescinded the first faith,"—that (faith), to wit, by which they were "found" in widowhood, and, after professing it, do not persevere. For which reason he "wills" them to "marry," for fear of their subsequently rescinding the first faith of professed widowhood; not to sanction their marrying as often as ever they may refuse to persevere in a widowhood plied with temptation—nay, rather, spent in indulgence.

"We read him withal writing to the Romans: 'But the woman who is under a husband, is bound to her husband (while) living; but if he shall have died, she has been emancipated from the law of the husband.' Doubtless, then, the husband living, she will be thought to commit adultery if she shall have been joined to a second husband. If, however, the husband shall have died, she has been freed from (his) law, (so) that she is not an adulteress if made (wife) to another husband." But read the sequel as well in order that this sense, which flatters you, may evade (your grasp). "And so," he says, "my brethren, be ye too made dead to the law through the body of Christ, that ye may be made (subject) to a second, —to Him, namely, who hath risen from the dead, that we may bear fruit to God. For when we were in the flesh, the passions of sin, which (passions) used to be efficiently caused through the law, (wrought) in our members unto the bearing of fruit to death; but now we have been emancipated from the law, being dead (to that) in which we used to be held, unto the serving of God in newness of spirit, and not in oldness of letter." Therefore, if he bids us "be made dead to the law through the body of Christ," (which is the Church, which consists in the spirit of newness,) not "through the letter of oldness," (that is, of the law,)—taking you away from the law, which does not keep a wife, when her husband is dead, from becoming (wife) to another husband—he reduces you to (subjection to) the contrary condition, that you are *not* to marry when you have lost your husband; and in as far as you would *not* be accounted an adulteress if you became (wife) to a second husband after the death of your (first) husband, if you were still bound to act in (subjection to) the law, in so far as a result of the diversity of (your) condition, he *does* prejudge you (guilty) of adultery if, after the death of your husband, you do marry another: inasmuch as you have now been made dead to the law, it cannot be lawful for you, now that you have withdrawn from that (law) in the eye of which it *was* lawful for you.

Chapter XIV. —Even If the Permission Had Been Given by St. Paul in the Sense Which the Psychics Allege, It Was Merely Like the Mosaic Permission of Divorce—A Condescension to Human Hard-Heartedness.

Now, if the apostle had even absolutely permitted marriage when one's partner has been lost *subsequently to* (conversion to) the faith, he would have done (it), just as (he did) the other (actions) which he did adversely to the (strict) letter of his own rule, to suit the circumstances of the times: circumcising Timotheus on account of "supposititious false brethren;" and leading certain "shaven men" into the temple on account of the observant watchfulness of the Jews—he who chastises the Galatians when they desire to live in (observance of) the law. But so did circumstances require him to "become all things to all, in order to gain all;" "travailing in birth with them until Christ should be formed in them;" and "cherishing, as it were a nurse," the little ones of faith, by teaching them some things "by way of indulgence, not by way of command"—for it is one thing to *indulge*, another to *bid*—permitting a temporary license of re-marriage on account of the "weakness of the flesh," just as Moses of divorcing on account of "the hardness of the heart."

And here, accordingly, we will render the supplement of this (his) meaning. For if Christ abrogated what Moses enjoined, because "from the beginning (it) was not so;" and (if)—this being so—Christ will not therefore be reputed to have come from some other Power; why may not the Paraclete, too, have abrogated an indulgence which Paul granted—

because second marriage withal "was not from the beginning"—without deserving on this account to be regarded with suspicion, as if he were an alien spirit, provided only that the super induction be worthy of God and of Christ? If it was worthy of God and of Christ to check "hard-heartedness" when the time (for its indulgence) was fully expired, why should it not be *more* worthy both of God and of Christ to shake off "infirmity of the flesh" when "the time" is already *more* "wound up?" If it is just that marriage be not severed, it is, of course, honorable too that it be not iterated. In short, in the estimation of the world, each is accounted a mark of good discipline: one under the name of concord; one, of modesty. "Hardness of heart" reigned till Christ's time; let "infirmity of the flesh" (be content to) have reigned till the time of the Paraclete. The New Law abrogated divorce—it had (somewhat) to abrogate; the New Prophecy (abrogates) second marriage, (which is) no less a divorce of the former (marriage). But the "hardness of heart" yielded to Christ more readily than the "infirmity of the flesh." The latter claims Paul in its own support more than the former Moses; if, indeed, it is claiming him in its support when it catches at his indulgence, (but) refuses his prescript—eluding his more deliberate opinions and his constant "wills," not suffering us to render to the apostle the (obedience) which he "prefers."

And how long will this most shameless "infirmity" persevere in waging a war of extermination against the "better things?" The time for its indulgence was (the interval) until the Paraclete began His operations, to whose coming were deferred by the Lord (the things) which in His day "could not be endured;" which it is now no longer competent for anyone to be unable to endure, seeing that He through whom the power of enduring is granted is not wanting. How long shall we allege "the flesh," because the Lord said, "the flesh is weak?" But He has withal premised that "the Spirit is prompt," in order that the Spirit may vanquish the flesh—that the weak may yield to the stronger. For again He says, "Let him who is able to receive,

receive (it);" that is, let him who is *not* able go his way. That rich man *did* go his way who had not "received" the precept of dividing his substance to the needy, and was abandoned by the Lord to his own opinion. Nor will "harshness" be on this account imputed to Christ, the ground of the vicious action of each individual free-will. "Behold," saith He, "I have set before thee good and evil." Choose that which is good: if you cannot, because you will not—for that you can if you will He has shown, because He has proposed each to your free-will—you ought to depart from Him whose will you do not.

Chapter XV. —Unfairness of Charging the Disciples of the New Prophecy with Harshness. The Charge Rather to Be Retorted Upon the Psychics.

What harshness, therefore, is here on our part, if we renounce (communion with) such as do not the will of God? What heresy, if we judge second marriage, as being unlawful, akin to adultery? For what is adultery but unlawful marriage? The apostle sets a brand upon those who were wont entirely to forbid marriage, who were wont at the same time to lay an interdict on meats which God has created. We, however, no more do away with marriage if we abjure its repetition, than we reprobate meats if we fast oftener (than others). It is one thing to do away with, another to regulate; it is one thing to lay down a law of not marrying, it is another to fix a limit to marrying. To speak plainly, if they who reproach us with harshness, or esteem heresy (to exist) in this (our) cause, foster the "infirmity of the flesh" to such a degree as to think it must have support accorded to it in frequency of marriage; why do they in another case neither accord it support nor foster it with indulgence—when, (namely), torments have reduced it to a denial (of the faith)? For, of course, that (infirmity) is more capable of excuse which has fallen in battle, than (that) which (has fallen) in the bed-chamber; (that) which has succumbed on the rack, than (that) which (has succumbed) on the bridal bed; (that) which has yielded to cruelty, than (that) which (has yielded) to appetite; that which has been overcome groaning, than (that) which (has been overcome) in heat. But the former they excommunicate, because it has not "endured unto the end:" the latter they prop up, as if withal it has "endured unto the end." Propose (the question) why each has not "endured unto the end;" and you will find the cause of that (infirmity) to be more honorable which has been unable to sustain savagery, than (of that) which (has been unable to sustain) modesty. And yet not even a blood wrung—not to say an immodest—defection does the "infirmity of the flesh" excuse!

Chapter XVI. —Weakness of the Pleas Urged in Defense of Second Marriage.

But I smile when (the plea of) "infirmity of the flesh" is advanced in opposition (to us: infirmity) which is (rather) to be called the height of strength. Iteration of marriage is an affair of strength: to rise again from the ease of continence to the works of the flesh, is (a thing requiring) substantial reins. Such "infirmity" is equal, to a third, and a fourth, and even (perhaps) a seventh marriage; as (being a thing) which increases its strength as often as its weakness; which will no longer have (the support of) an apostle's authority, but of some Hermogenes—wont to marry more women than he paints. For in him matter is abundant: whence he presumes that even the soul is material; and therefore much more (than other men) he has *not* the Spirit from God, being no longer even a Psychic, because even his psychic element is not derived from God's afflatus! What if a man allege "indigence," so as to profess that his flesh is openly prostituted, and given in marriage for the sake of maintenance; forgetting that there is to be no careful thought about food and clothing? He has God (to look to), the Foster-father even of ravens, the Rearer even of flowers. What if he plead the loneliness of his home? as if one woman afforded company to a man ever on the eve of flight!

He has, of course, a widow (at hand), whom it will be lawful for him to take. Not one such wife, but even a plurality, it is permitted to have. What if a man thinks on posterity, with thoughts like the eyes of Lot's wife; so that a man is to make the fact that from his former marriage he has had no children a reason for repeating marriage? A Christian, forsooth, will seek heirs, disinherited as he is from the entire world! He has "brethren;" he has the Church as his mother. The case is different if men believe that, at the bar of Christ as well (as of Rome), action is taken on the principle of the Julian laws; and imagine that the unmarried and childless cannot receive their portion in full, in accordance with the testament of God. Let such (as thus think), then, marry to the very end; that in this confusion of flesh they, like Sodom and Gomorrah, and the day of the deluge, may be overtaken by the fated final end of the world. A third saying let them add, "Let us eat, and drink, *and marry*, for to-morrow we shall die;" not reflecting that the "woe" (denounced) "on such as are with child, and are giving suck," will fall far more heavily and bitterly in the "universal shaking" of the entire world than it did in the devastation of one fraction of Judæa. Let them accumulate by their iterated marriages fruits right seasonable for the last times—breasts heaving, and wombs qualmish, and infants whimpering. Let them prepare for Antichrist (children) upon whom he may more passionately (than Pharaoh) spend his savagery. He will lead to them murderous midwives.

Chapter XVII. —Heathen Examples Cry Shame Upon This "Infirmity of the Flesh."

They will have plainly a specious privilege to plead before Christ—the everlasting "infirmity of the flesh!" But upon this (infirmity) will sit in judgment no longer an Isaac, our monogamist father; or a John, a noted voluntary celibate of Christ's; or a Judith, daughter of Merari; or so many other examples of saints. Heathens are wont to be destined our judges. There will arise a queen of Carthage, and give sentence upon the Christians, who, refugee as she was, living on alien soil, and at that very time the originator of so mighty a state, whereas she ought unasked to have craved royal nuptials, yet, for fear she should experience a second marriage, preferred on the contrary rather to "burn" than to "marry." Her assessor will be the Roman matron who, having—albeit it was through noctural violence, nevertheless—known another man, washed away with blood the stain of her flesh, that she might avenge upon her own person (the honor of) monogamy. There have been, too, who preferred to die for their husbands rather than marry after their husbands' death. To idols, at all events, both monogamy and widowhood serve as apparitors. On Fortuna Muliebris, as on Mother Matuta, none but a once wedded woman hangs the wreath. Once for all do the Pontifex Maximus and the wife of a Flamen marry. The priestesses of Ceres, even during the lifetime and with the consent of their husbands, are widowed by amicable separation. There are, too, who may judge us on the ground of absolute continence: the virgins of Vesta, and of the Achaian Juno, and of the Scythian Diana, and of the Pythian Apollo. On the ground of continence, the priests likewise of the famous Egyptian bull will judge the "infirmity" of Christians. Blush, O flesh, who hast "put on" Christ! Suffice it thee once for all to marry, whereto "from the beginning" thou was created, whereto by "the end" thou art being recalled! Return at least to the former Adam, if to the last thou canst not! Once for all did he taste of the tree; once for all felt concupiscence; once for all veiled his shame; once for all blushed in the presence of God; once for all concealed his guilty hue; once for all was exiled from the paradise of holiness; once for all thenceforward married. If you were "in him," you have your norm; if you have passed over "into Christ," you will be bound to be (yet) better. Exhibit (to us) a third Adam, and him a digamist; and then you will be able to be what, between the two, you cannot.

Elucidations.

I.

(About 160 years having elapsed, pp. 59, 61.)

If the First Epistle to the Corinthians was written a.d. 57, and if our author speaks with designed precision, and not in round numbers, the date of this treatise should be a.d. 217—a date which I should prefer to accept. Bishop Kaye, however, instances capp. 7 and 9 in the *Ad Nationes* as proving his disposition to give his numbers in loose rhetoric, and not with arithmetical accuracy. Pamelius, on the other hand, gives a.d. 213.

On the general subject Kaye bids us read cap. 3, with cap. 14, to grasp the argument of our enthusiast. In few words, our author holds that St. Paul condescends to human infirmity in permitting any marriage whatever, pointing to a better way. The apostle himself says, "The time is short;" but a hundred and sixty years have passed since then, and why may not the Spirit of truth and righteousness now, after so long a time, be given to animate the adult Church to that which is pronounced the better way in Scripture itself?

Our author seems struggling here, according to my view, with his own rule of *prescription.* He would free the doctrine from the charge of novelty by pointing it out in the Scripture of a hundred and sixty years before. But how instinctively the Church ruled against this sophistry, condemning in advance that whole system of "development" which a modern Tertullian defends on grounds quite as specious, under a Montanistic subjection that makes a Priscilla of the Roman pontiff. Let me commend the reader to the remarks upon Tertullian of the "judicious Hooker," in book ii. capp. v. 5, 6; also book iv. cap. vii. 4, 5, and elsewhere.

II.

(Abrogated indulgence (comp. capp. 2 and 3), p. 70.)

Poor Tertullian is at war with himself in all the works which he indites against Catholic orthodoxy. In the tract *De Exhort. Castitatis* he gives one construction to 1 Cor. ix. 5, which in this he explains away; and now he patches up his conclusion by referring to his Montanistic "Paraclete." In fighting Marcion, how thoroughly he agrees with Clement of Alexandria as to the sanctity of marriage. In the second epistle to his wife, how beautiful his tribute to the married state, blessed by the Church, and enjoyed in chastity. But here how fanatically he would make out that marriage is but tolerated adultery! From Tertullian himself we may prove the marriage of the clergy, and that (*de Exhort. Cast.*, last chapter) abstinence was voluntary and exceptional, however praiseworthy. Also, if he here urges that (cap. 12) even laymen should abstain from second marriages, he allows the liberty of the clergy to marry once. He admits St. Peter's marriage. Eusebius proves the marriage of St. Jude. Concerning "the grave dignity" of a single marriage, we may concede that Tertullian proves his point, but no further.

In England the principles of the *Monogamia* were revived by the eccentric Whiston (*circa* a.d. 1750), and attracted considerable attention among the orthodox,—a fact pleasantly satirized by Goldsmith in his *Vicar of Wakefield*.

On the general subject comp. Chrysost., tom. iii. p. 226: "Laus Maximi, et quales ducendæ sint uxores."

www.ingramcontent.com/pod-product-compliance
Lightning Source LLC
Chambersburg PA
CBHW071014120726
47910CB00004B/1521

* 9 7 8 1 6 4 3 7 3 0 9 5 0 *